Spring 2014

Studio Report

Another Nature

When considering the "nature" of architecture today, isn't it problematic to simply define it as an "artifact" or "artificial environment" that is conceived and constructed specifically for people?

From such a constrained point of view, we'll find it impossible to resolve any of the widespread problems that face us. Instead, isn't it necessary that we consider architecture from a broader perspective?

Rather than limiting our understanding of architecture as an environment for people, we need to foster an awareness of contemporary issues that incorporates all aspects of our surroundings.

Thinking beyond the scale and implications of the conventional artificial environments that we find in buildings, landscapes, and urban designs, in this studio we considered an expanded notion of architecture that meets the demands of today's society.

Instructor
Junya Ishigami

Teaching Associate
Sky Milner

Students
Joon Hyuk Choe, Yun Fu, Jerome Hord, Emily Kappes, Gunho Kim, Quyen Luu, Matthew Montry, Kevin Murray, Patricia Semmler, Jiasi Tan, Chenyao Tang, Yuhui Xu

Midterm Critics
Mitsuhiro Kanada, Tetsuo Kondo, Ryue Nishizawa, Jun Sato, Kazuyo Sejima

Final Review Critics
Hitoshi Abe, Anton Abril-garcia, Silvia Benedito, Mark Lee, Peter Rose, Maryann Thompson

Introduction

Projects

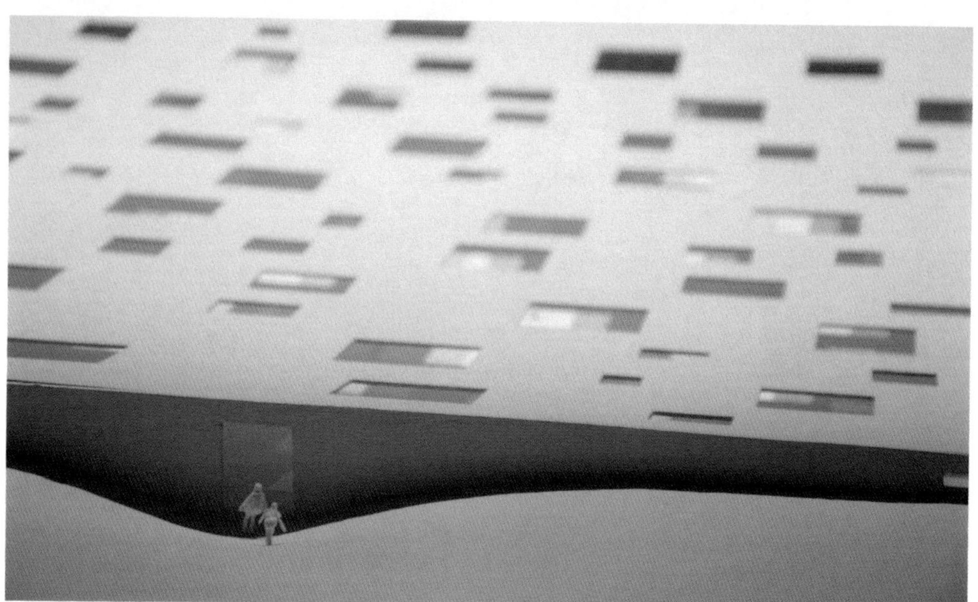

junya.ishigami + associates, model of entrance to KAIT Cafe.

In my practice, we endeavor to contemplate two fundamental aspects of architecture: comfort and constructivity.

New Comfort

Until recently, architecture sought to segregate humans from nature, through shelter, with an artificially created "comfortable" environment. Today the distinction between natural and manmade environments is becoming ambiguous, and new environments are emerging. For these new environments, a new theory of architecture is needed, one that goes beyond the shelter concept. I believe it is very important to think about how people can find comfort and how we can define a "new comfort" in architecture.

New Constructivity

Conceiving of ways to build structures has been one of the critical tasks of architecture from time immemorial. We feel that exploring new approaches to construction in architecture that transcend and overturn conventional concepts can be a means of expanding the possibilities of architecture. During our time, the range of our values has become much wider than before. To respond to this diversity and devise various new approaches to construction, it is necessary to think freely and flexibly of architecture. We maintain that considering a new method for independent architectural design, both technically and conceptually, can be the most significant step to take now.

Through the process of exploring these two components of architecture beyond their known limits, we intend to take conventional practice in another direction, both physically and conceptually, and to continue testing the possibilities of new architecture today.

—Junya Ishigami
2014 Kenzo Tange Visiting Chair in Architecture and Urban Design

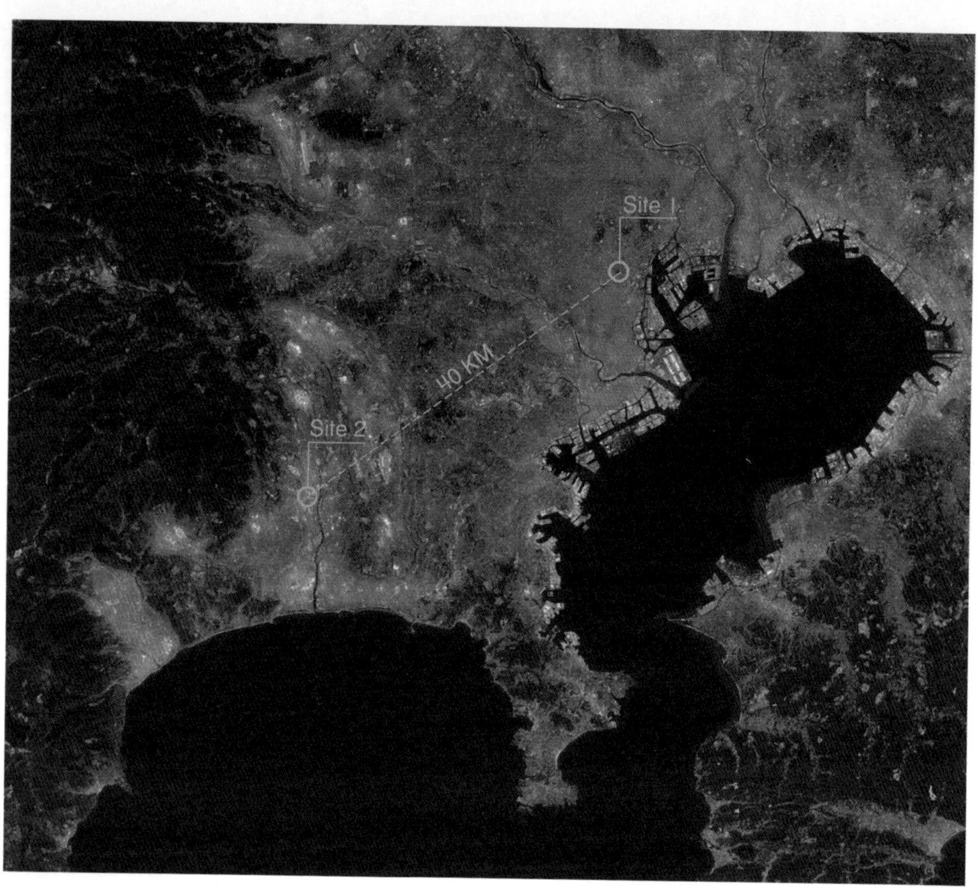

Satellite image of the Tokyo Metropolitan Region, Japan.

Another Nature invited new views on place and the role of architecture, challenging the distinctions created through program, enclosure, and formal organization. Our studio considered these relationships in the context of contemporary Tokyo, a city where rapid and extensive urbanization has increasingly alienated individuals from their natural surroundings. Considered among the densest regions in the world, the larger Tokyo metropolitan area has well over 35 million inhabitants, with urban buildup extending uninterrupted to the surrounding foothills. Although the country as a whole is relatively affluent, it faces persistent economic stagnation compounded by an aging population, rising state expenditures, and a diminishing tax base. These larger issues call into question existing approaches toward development and provide an opening for new conceptions of building and public space.

The studio focused on two sites:

Site 1: The Tokyo Metropolitan Teien Art Museum in central Tokyo. This seemingly idyllic park grounds and abutting nature reserve have been carefully maintained and preserved from encroaching urban development. Currently, the museum is undergoing renovations to reestablish its prominence as a cultural institution and increase visitorship.

Site 2: The Atsugi city bus terminal, a transit hub near the main train station of Atsugi, is located in Atsugi, Kanagawa, a commuter town roughly 40 kilometers southwest of central Tokyo. The 1-hectare bus terminal is covered by an underutilized elevated public plaza. The city is considering redevelopment in the hopes that it will increase downtown activity.

These two sites and their surroundings have contrasting relationships when considered within the context of the larger metropolitan region. The first is a preserved natural park isolated from its urban context in the center of Tokyo. The second is a neglected urban pocket in a declining city in the urban hinterland. Both sites will benefit from creative approaches toward revitalization that create new meaningful experiences and places for visitors. Each of the following projects develops unique architectural sensibilities and expressions that address these site-specific relationships.

Site 1: Tokyo Metropolitan Teien Art Museum

The Teien Metropolitan Museum is located on a 3.75-hectare park ground in Meguro, Tokyo. Throughout the last century the site was preserved from encroaching urban development as a semi-natural space, partly due to its use as the imperial residence of Prince Asaka Yasuhiko during the beginning of the century. In 1962 the southwest portion of the site was altered to make way for an elevated highway (route 2), and while it remains an important pocket of green space in the neighborhood, it is increasingly isolated from the surrounding commercial and community activity. The museum is currently under renovation to reinvent itself as a contemporary cultural institution with larger appeal to residents throughout Tokyo. As part of this effort, the southern portion of the park grounds is being reconsidered as an inviting space that incorporates a cafe and possibly other public amenities. The sensitive nature of the site, including a restriction on substantial excavation due to archeological evidence dating back to the early settlements of the Jomon period, make introducing new functions a challenge.

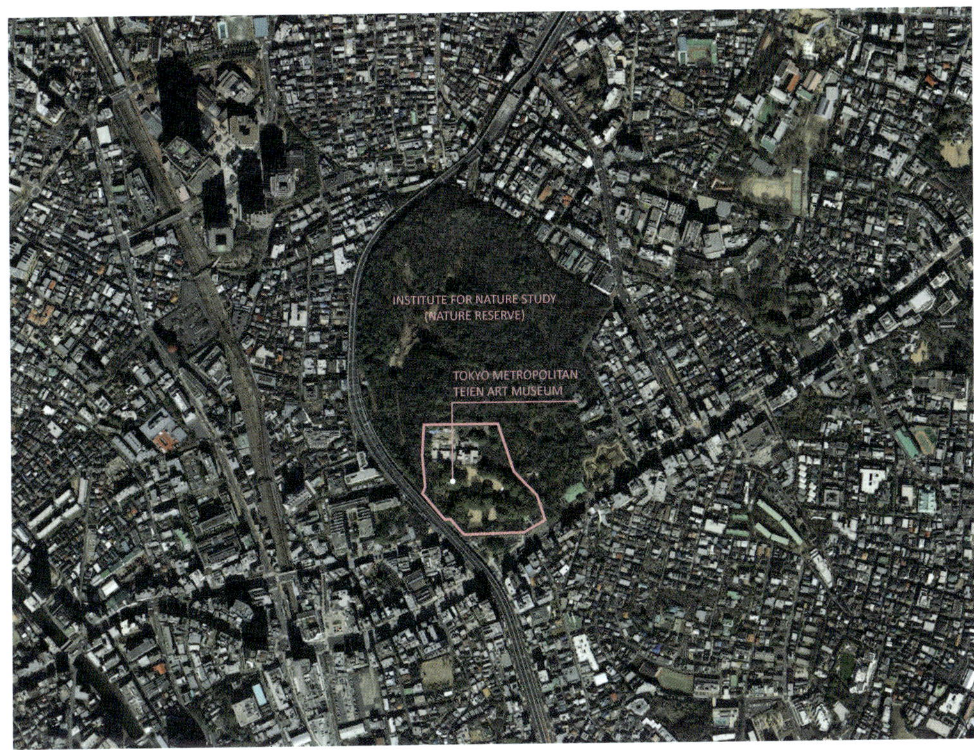

Aerial image of site.

1909

1921

1955

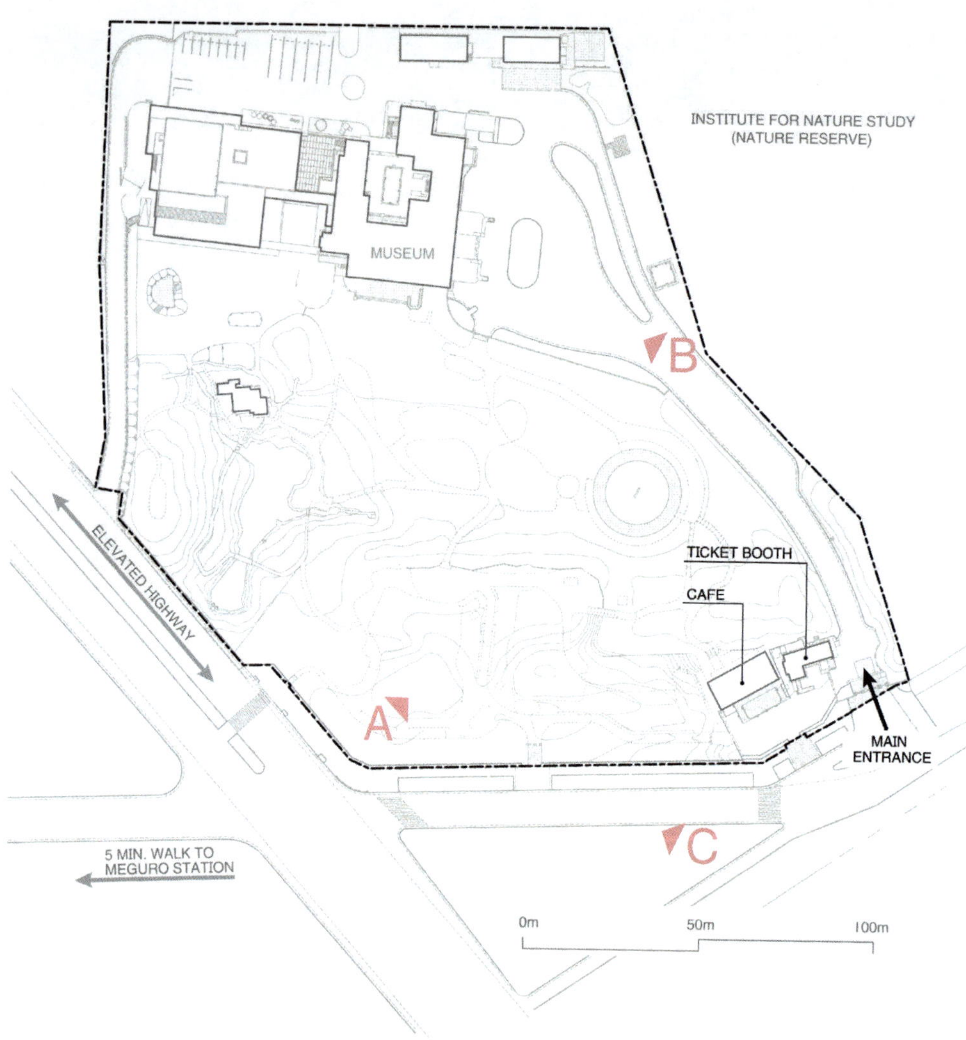
INSTITUTE FOR NATURE STUDY
(NATURE RESERVE)
MUSEUM
B
ELEVATED HIGHWAY
TICKET BOOTH
CAFE
A
MAIN
ENTRANCE
C
5 MIN. WALK TO
MEGURO STATION
0m
50m
100m

View of the site from three locations.

Tokyo Metropolitan Teien Art Museum

Edge of Nature

Joon Hyuk Choe

Another Nature means a new way of perceiving what is natural—in other words, a new norm or a new typology for a given site condition. Thus the project claims to propose a new typological approach to hard edge conditions in the city today.

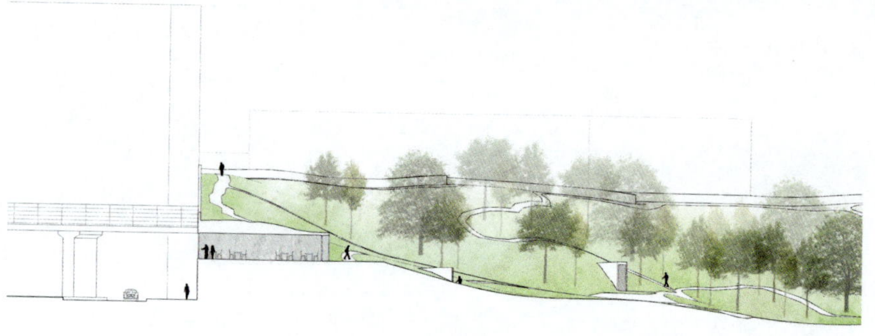

The project explores a problematic boundary between the Teien Park and the elevated highway that runs along the western perimeter. This infrastructure establishes a hard edge that separates the nature within the park from the urban fabric of Meguro, contaminating the natural experience with the sight and sounds of the highway.

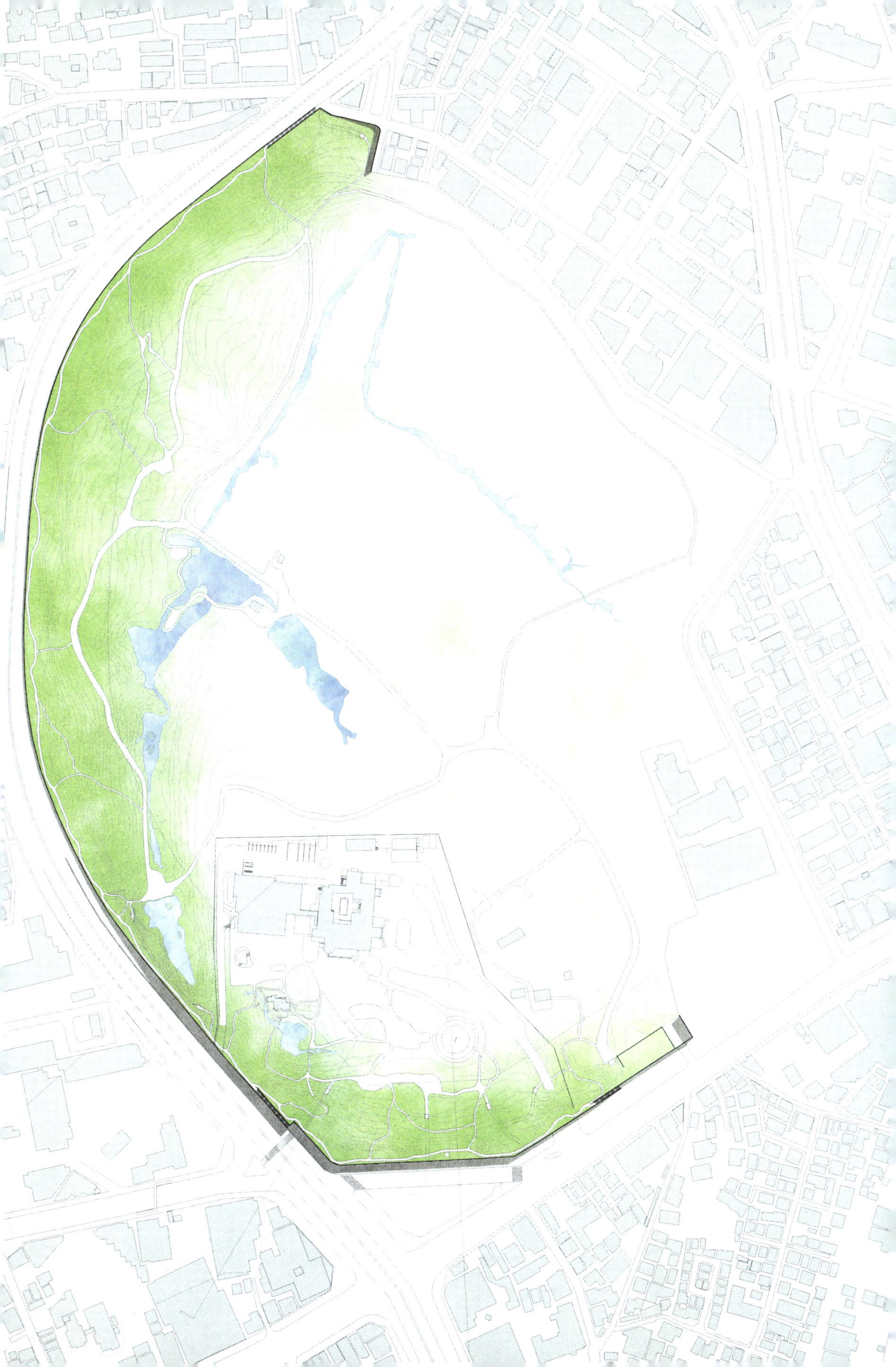

To resolve this conflict, the edge of the park is proposed to rise up by 15 meters, terminating as a solid wall that faces the city.

By mounding up the western edge, the park is protected from the highway and the occupants are able to enjoy an uninterrupted natural experience. Climbing the mound elevates the occupant to a view of the rooftops of the adjacent neighborhood, heightening the significance of nature in the context of Meguro.

House for Plants

Jiasi Tan

I feel that the relationship between humans and nature is unfair, as it appears that everything is designed for human beings. From urban planners to architects, they place humans at the center. They never carefully design a natural space. It seems that humans are at the center of everything artificial or non-artificial. We should not be so anthropocentric.

Human beings and nature shouldn't occupy an unspoken hierarchy: the natural environment and human beings are on an equal footing. I made the "House for Plants" to encourage human beings to treat nature as an equal.

In this project, I tried to treat a natural environment the same way that we treat human beings: study the plants and see what's the best scale and shape for the "House for Plants."

The park is totally isolated from the surrounding environment. The fences and the highway—everything is blocking the park from the urban environment. I think that all of the plants here were just given a piece of land to live in, not provided a carefully designed space.

If the park is carefully designed, and if the plants have their own houses in the air according to their varied scales, habits, and demands for sunlight, water, air, and space, all problems will be solved.

After carefully studying various scales and demands within a living environment, I designed the "House for Plants." Sections have different scales, shapes, and environments according to varied plants' multiple demands.

The Sky Garden attracts more birds, which are seed-dispersal agents. The diagram draws relationships between vegetation on site and seed-dispersal agents. The tiny world I created is not only for human beings, it's for all natural elements: animals, birds, and plants as well as humans.

Scale of Nature

Jerome Hord

Another Nature has to challenge both the perception of and the dependence on the human scale. The sequoias of Northern California overtake our concept of self, while the banyan trees of the tropics speak to the blurring of the individual and the notion that perhaps the whole can be greater than the sum of its parts.

As city dwellers, we misdiagnose what nature is. No longer do we desire to differentiate between the natural and the artificial, for nature has found its place within the streetscape of artificial signs and symbols that permeate our everyday lives.

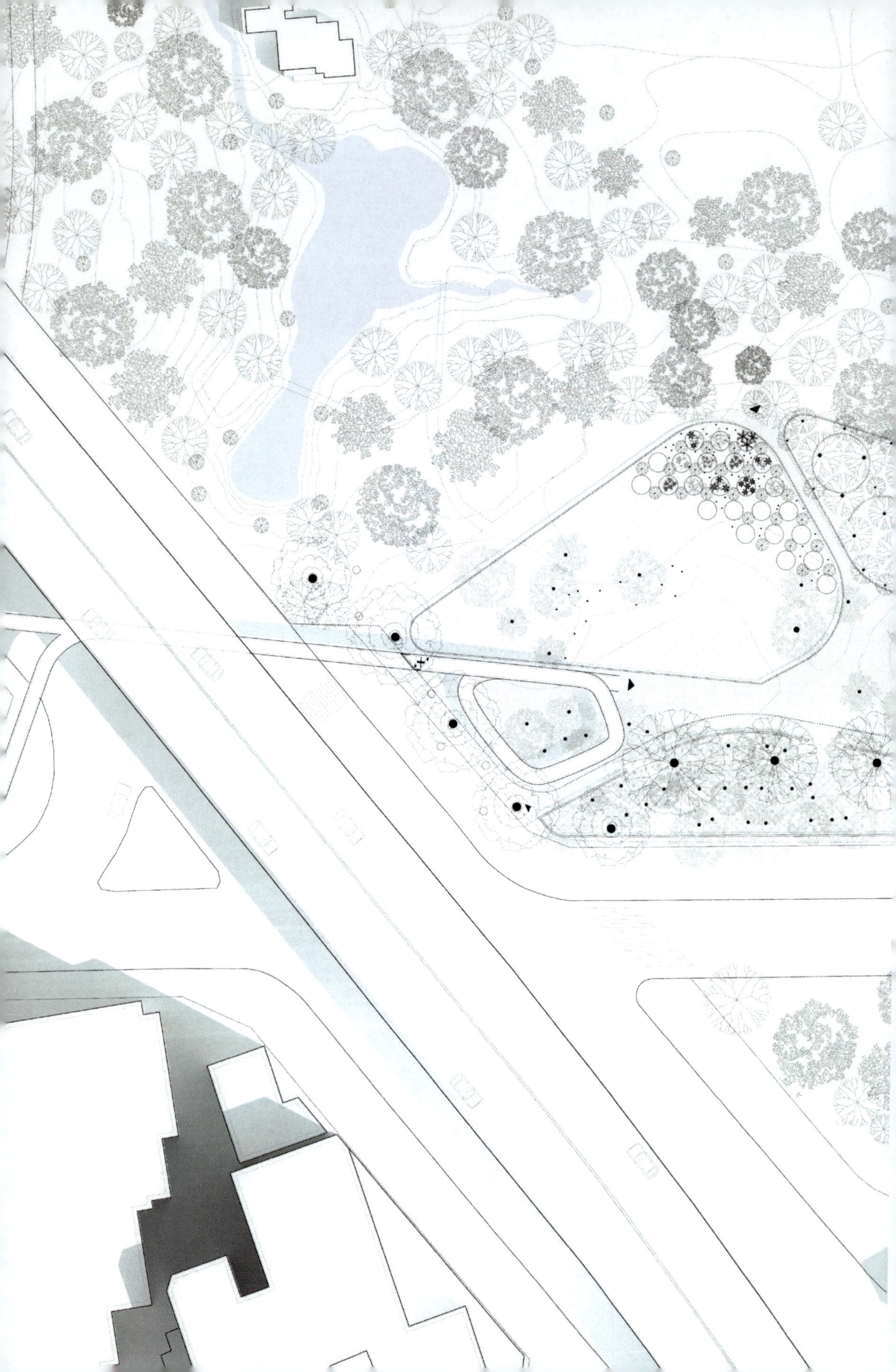

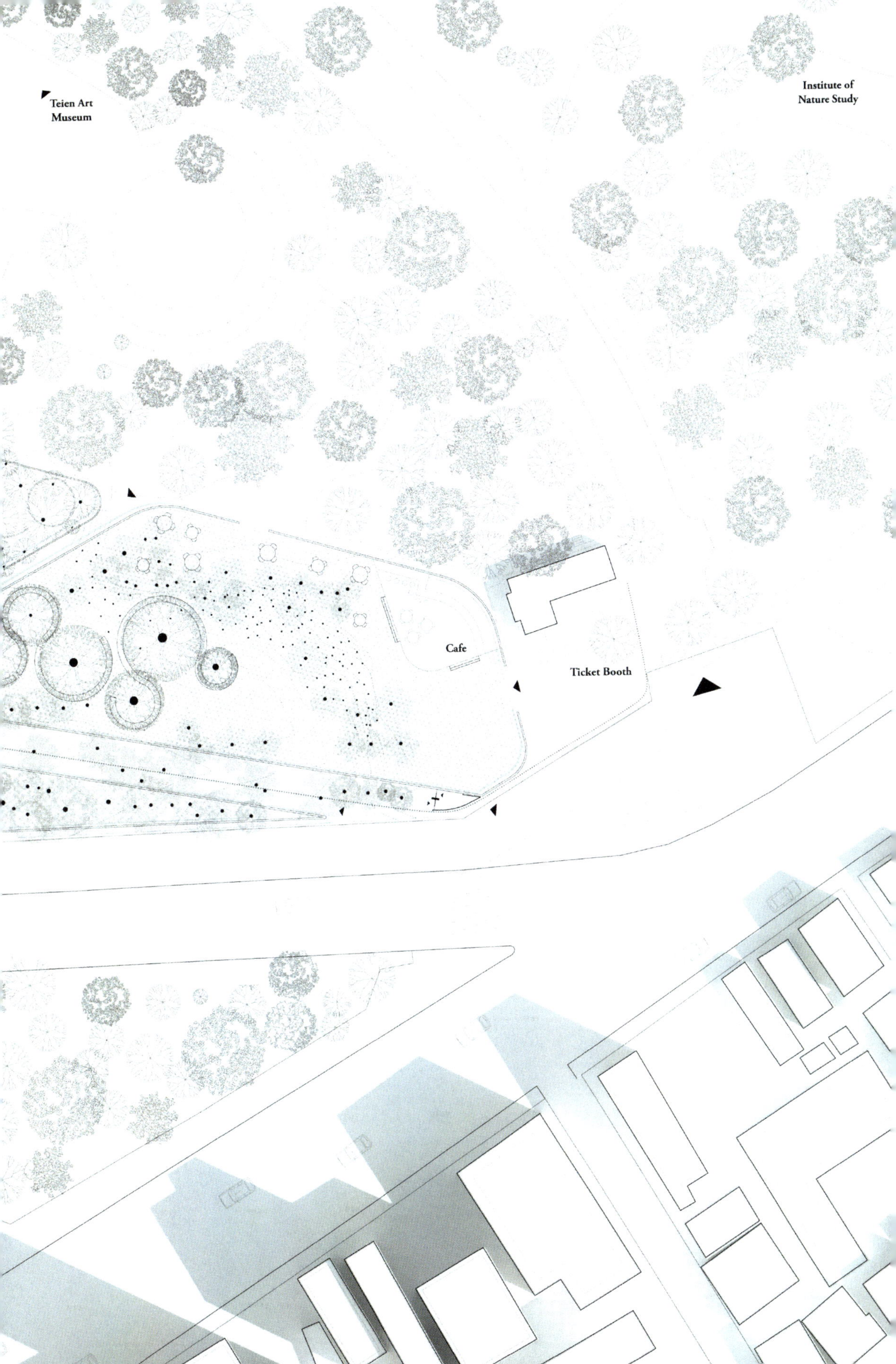
Teien Art Museum
Institute of Nature Study
Cafe
Ticket Booth

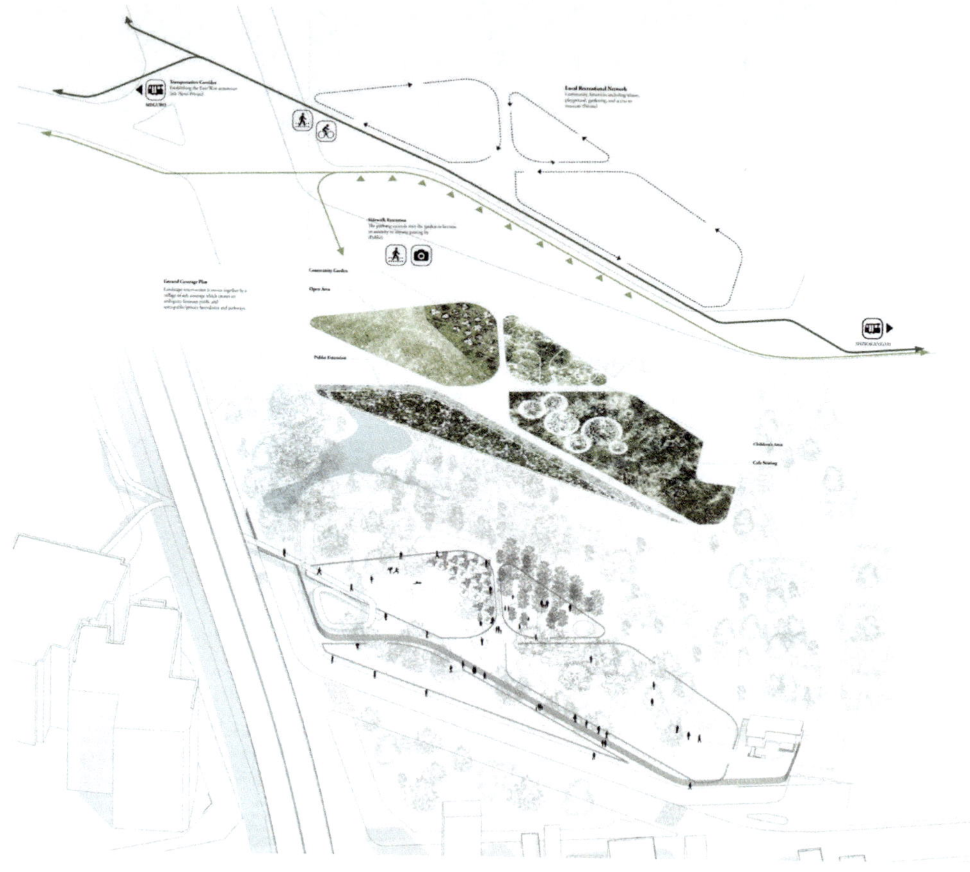

The various trees and shrubs that line the street act as mere indicators of what nature is supposed to be and only serve as a reminder that just maybe, nature is a thing that exists—while its function has been reduced to simple performative techniques. In the city, the sidewalk is where we experience this quasi nature.

We notice immediately that the scale of this nature hardly reacts to its surroundings and only to the perception of man, for it is designed to accommodate only the human scale. It almost never responds to the surrounding dense urban fabric.

Median Landscape

Kevin Murray

The site at Teien, a median divided from the park by the development of an underground train in the late 1990s, sits among roadways, an overpass, pedestrian traffic, and bicycle lanes. The median remains zoned as protected park space although it is no longer held within the perimeter gate of the Teien Museum grounds.

Reconsideration of the median itself as a gate between roadway and greenspace, public and private, and urban and infinite allows the intervention to engage Another Nature, negotiating infrastructure not as a groundscape of fragmentation but as a patchwork of layers and seams.

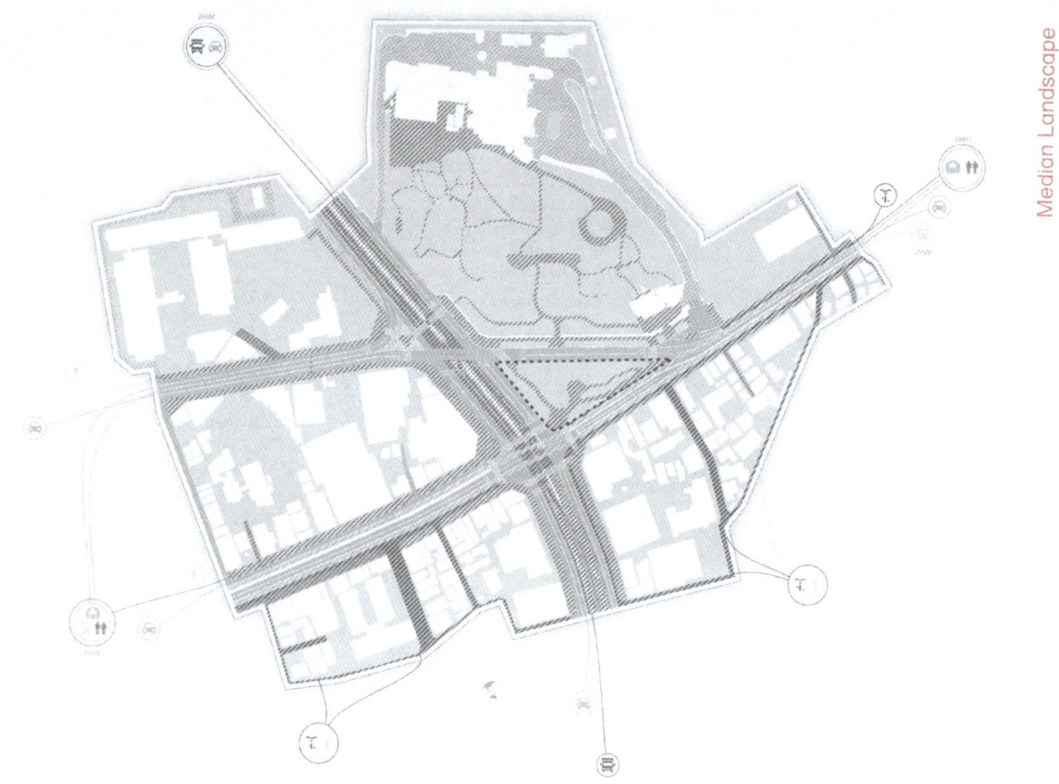

The attrition of the Japanese landscape through political boundaries, religious right, and transitory modernization has neglected small urban voids.

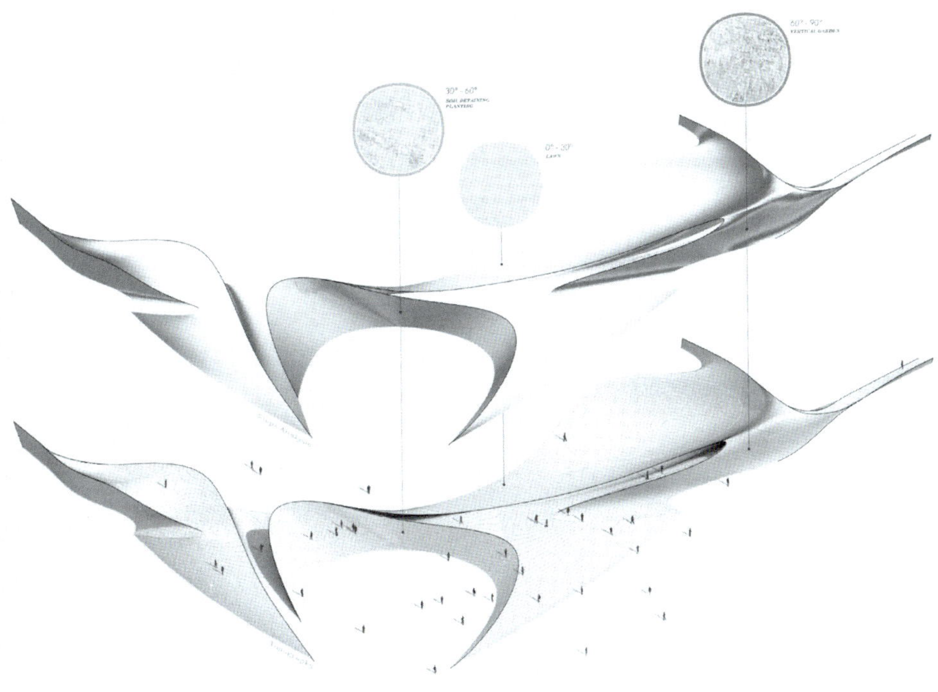

By either nostalgia or accident, these spaces—more commonly known as street medians—are heavily curated to represent shards of a broken singularity that once unified the landscape of Japan.

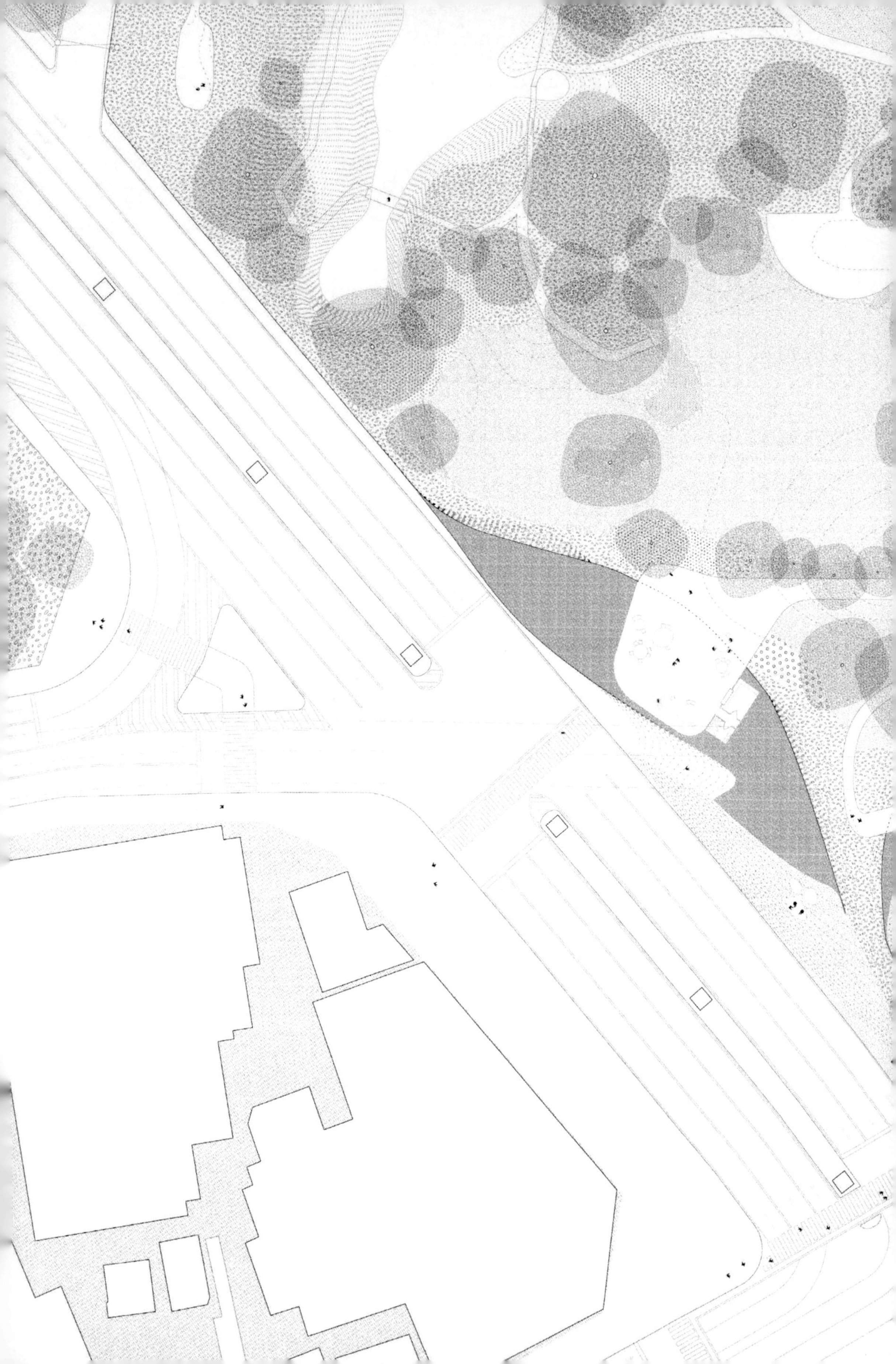

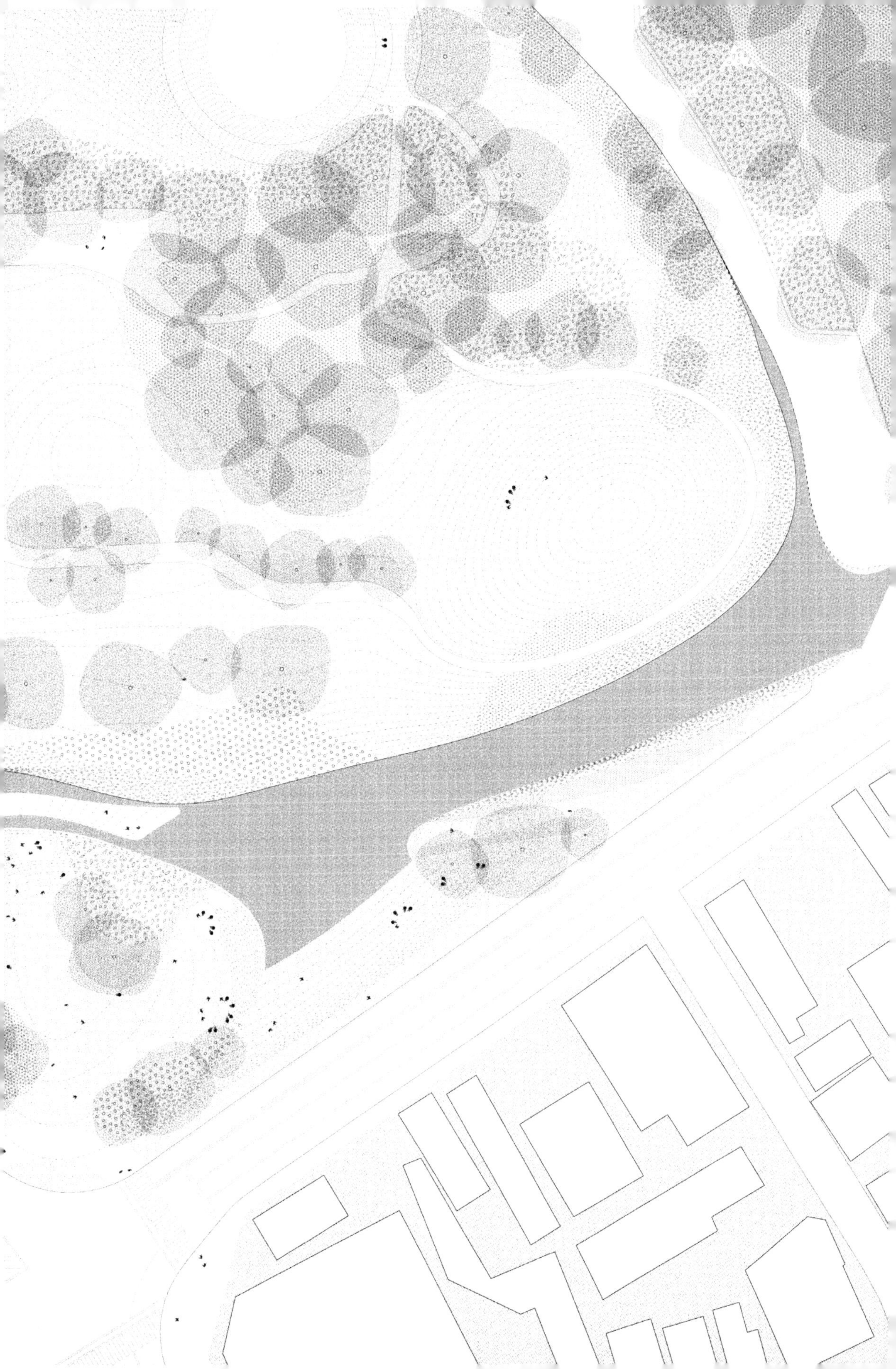

Through canted planes and rolling lawns, the project engages the rise and fall of the landscape as a method to create soft boundaries and blended programmatic uses.

The urban layering of infrastructure becomes not a learned social code but a haptic experience.

Cycle of Changes

Patricia Semmler

Another Nature for me is a new architecture that is part of the natural cycle of changes; it is unexpected and welcomes beauty. The building integrates the path of the sun, direction of the wind, and rain and snow at its center. Trees grow in its columns to feed the birds. A birdhouse is set up on top of the previous ticket building, which becomes an outside space. The path through the building allows views to the birds' spaces and places to sit, read, eat, or gather.

The idea of nature speaks to both the unmediated physical world that surrounds us and the inherent character of a person or thing—its essence.

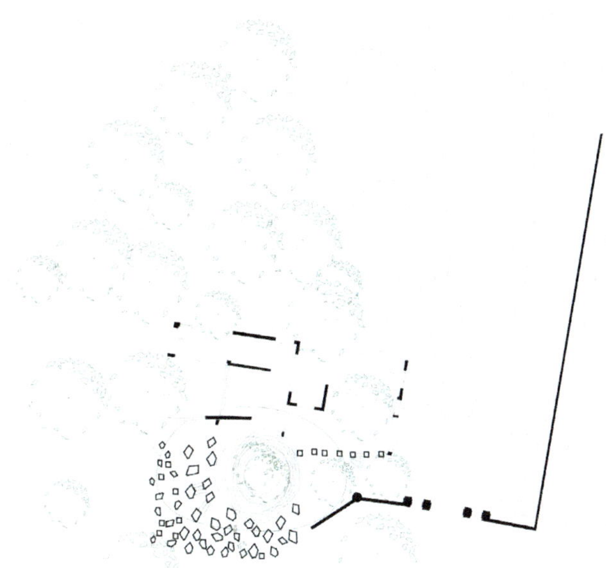

To me, Another Nature calls for a renewed way of thinking of nature, our natural environment, in relationship to the built environment. More important, I understand it as a challenge to define "another nature" for architecture, to rethink the very essence of this discipline.

This project aims to create an architecture that is inspired by nature, an architecture that is part of nature, by incorporating the changes in the environment that challenge the distinction between architecture and nature, human and animal, and by taking into account all living beings in its design.

The building is organized in two main parts, in dialogue with its surroundings; the columns face the city and filter views and people, and the "skeleton" shapes spaces, defining indoor in outdoor, while allowing the trees to be part of these spaces.

The building's shape and organization aim to be open to the unexpected, but also propose spaces that can be seen differently every time. The complexity works to make the person who visits attentive to the space, even if only subconsciously.

The building is not only used but felt, and through the feelings that it gives to the those who pass through, the building comes into existence.

New Path, New Topography

Chenyao Tang

The project aims to explore the relationship between path and topography in both natural and artificial contexts.

The concept is to connect existing objects (main art museum, Japanese tea house, pond, sculpture) by applying a new path. Visitors can explore the environment in an unexpected way during the path's merging and meandering with the topography.

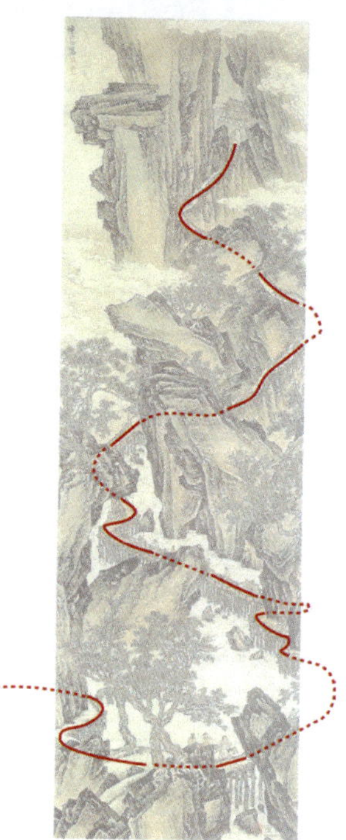

Xie Shichen, *Landscape of Jiange in Sichuan*, Ming Dynasty, 132.5 x 40 inches.

My proposal is to employ new topography, combining wavy and flat areas. Risen and sunken terrains are created to make a boundary and define space.

Two contrastive spaces are created: linear space, defined by the path, and group space, enclosed by small hills. The two spaces are where various activities happen.

Artificial land is carefully organized with natural land, merging with the route.

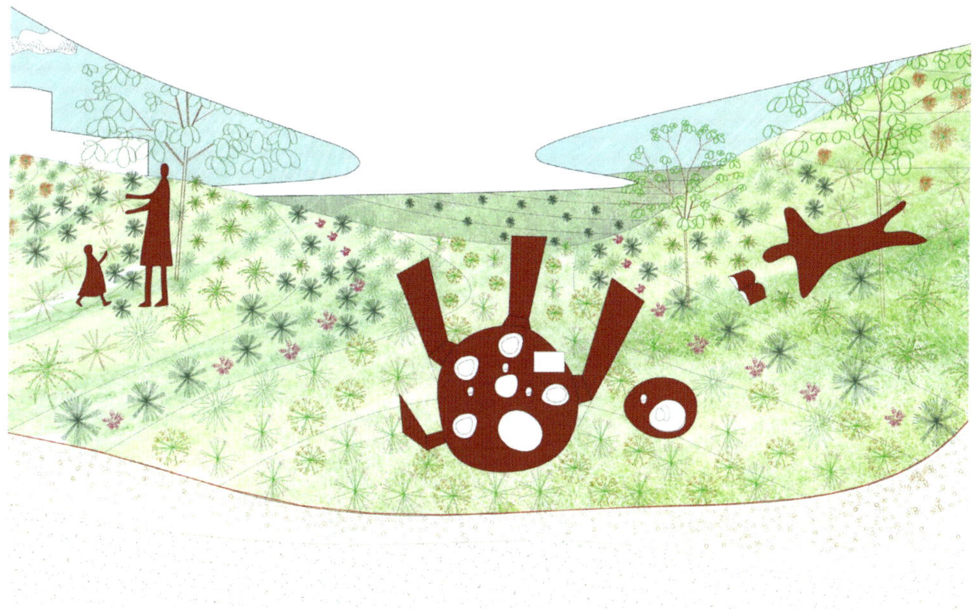

The terrain of Japanese gardens is very interesting; in most Western gardens terrain is relatively flat.

Site 2: Atsugi City Bus Terminal

The Atsugi city bus terminal is located in Atsugi, Kanagawa, a commuter town of over 220,000 residents roughly 40 kilometers southwest of central Tokyo. The site is located within a five-minute walk from Atsugi train station and is heavily trafficked by commuters working in Tokyo. Over the last several decades, downtown Atsugi's local businesses have been in decline despite the great amount of traffic filtering through the terminal. In the hopes of providing a communal "third space" for residents to linger, the publicly owned bus terminal site is slated for redevelopment as part of the city's urban revitalization plan. In addition to the existing bus terminal, the proposed new civic space may incorporate the adjacent library and commercial program. Given its prominent location near the elevated Odakyu train line, the new development will act as an icon for the city in the eyes of commuters.

Aerial view of downtown Atsugi.

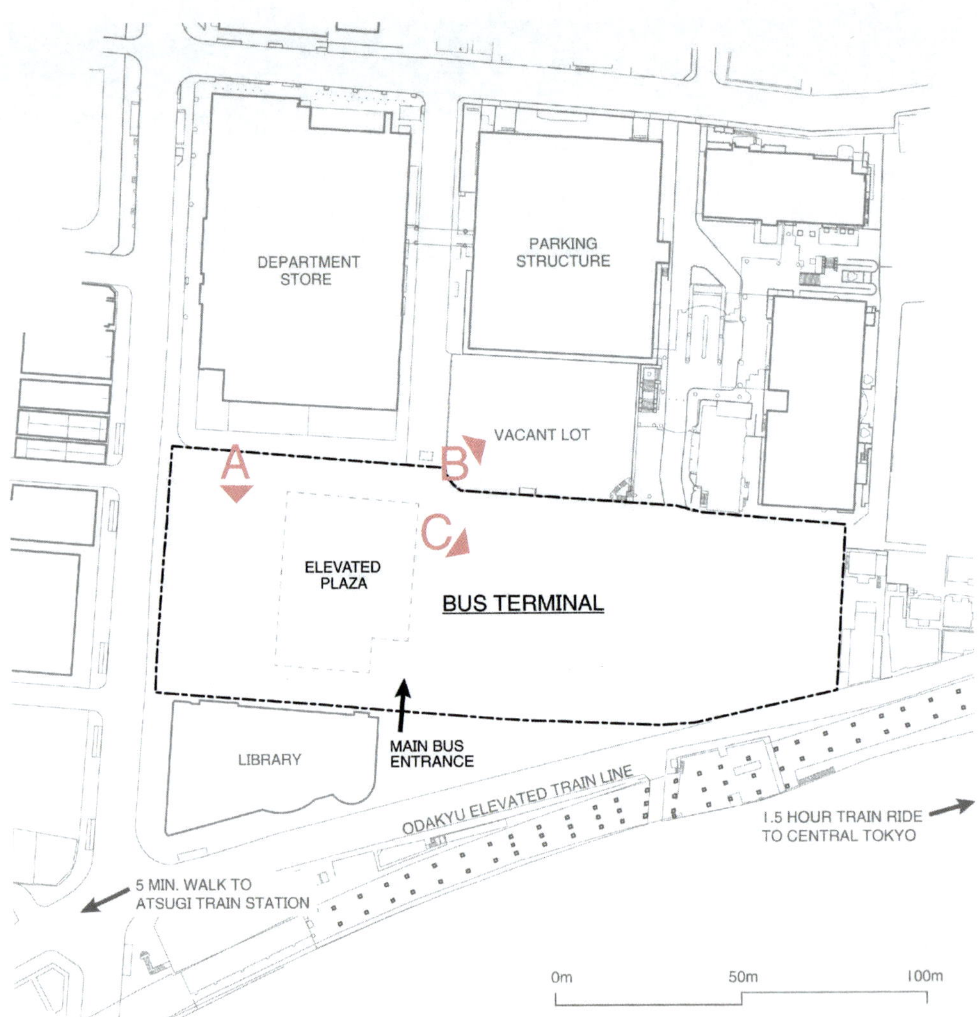
DEPARTMENT STORE
PARKING STRUCTURE
VACANT LOT
A
B
C
ELEVATED PLAZA
BUS TERMINAL
LIBRARY
MAIN BUS ENTRANCE
ODAKYU ELEVATED TRAIN LINE
1.5 HOUR TRAIN RIDE TO CENTRAL TOKYO
5 MIN. WALK TO ATSUGI TRAIN STATION
0m
50m
100m

View of the site from three locations.

Atsugi Station Bus Terminal

The Episodic Landscape of the Street

Emily Kappes

When we are in nature, we have a collective experience. This is something that everyone can relate to. Another Nature to me is the collective experience of space that is more than just functional; it allows us to connect as people, just as we do in nature. An important way to do this is through scale: something large reminds us that we are small. A building can be designed not for humans but for hills.

Kan Tsunenobu, *Scene from the Tale of Genji*, six-panel screen, ca. 1677, 67 x 145 inches.

Atsugi is a city with no mystery. The suburban condition is polarized between public space and private space, lacking semi-private medium-scale social spaces.

Although the site is large—the size of many urban blocks—the project is one design and one building. It cannot pretend to be the same as the old Japanese city that was formed by the aggregation of irregular lots over time. This project seeks to evoke the playful, episodic nature of the traditional Japanese street without duplicating it in form.

In the Japanese city, the buildings structure the landscape into streets. In this new urbanism, the buildings shape the landscape into streets not just in plan but also in section. Concrete walls retain the earth, lifting it up and over the buildings. A variety of interior and exterior spaces are created by an open network of structural planes.

The building crafts two narrative streets—one at ground level serves the library and bus station, and another rises up, acting as a community strolling garden with vistas into a variety of courts and onto the city. Like the old Japanese city, streets bring together individual experiences and distant captured views into a single story.

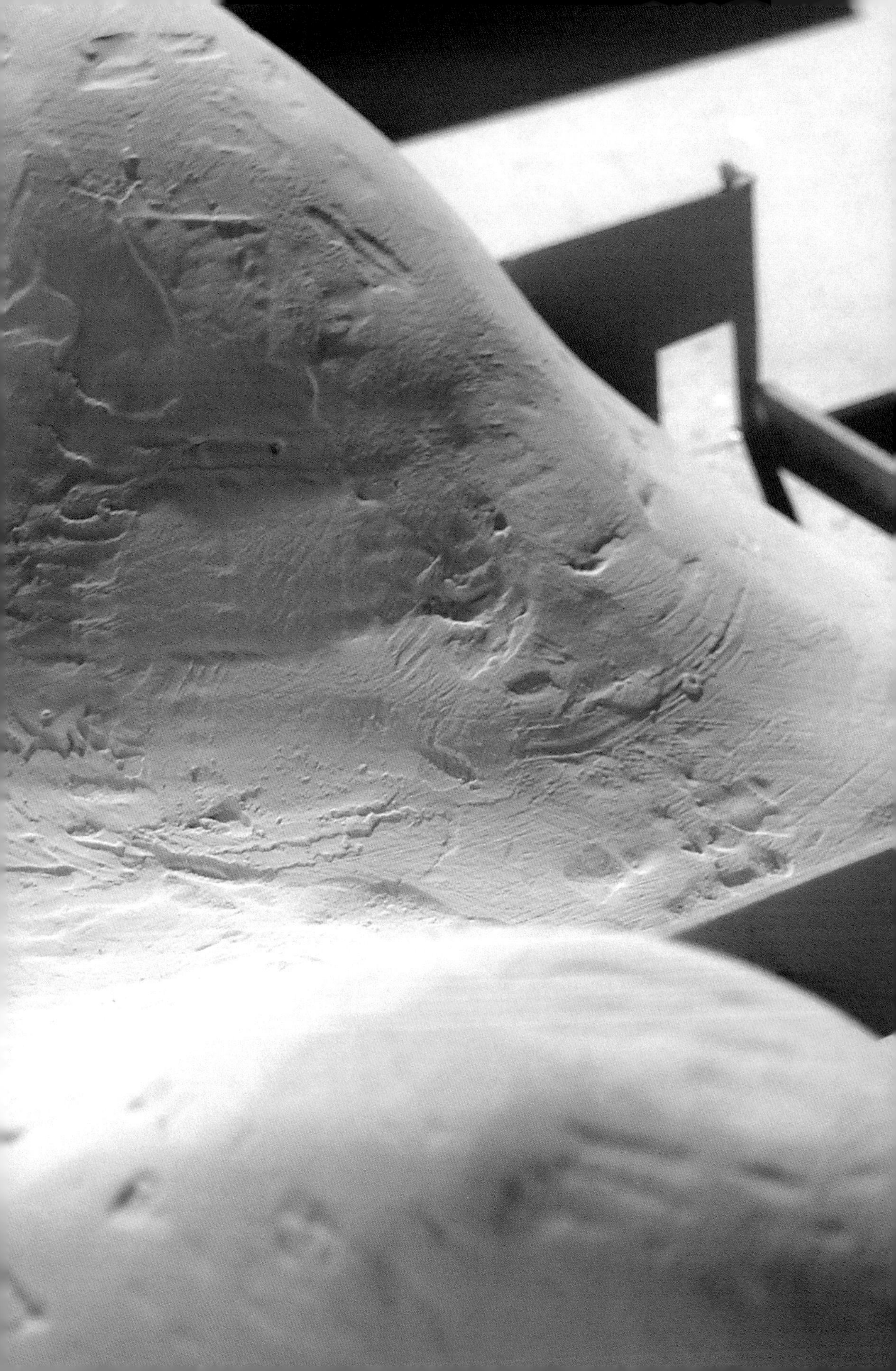

Funicular Library

Yun Fu

Japan is an earthquake nation, with a building culture strongly influenced by seismic risk. In the modern context, the architectural language is closely associated with approaches to structural design. Seven distinct structural typologies can be observed in modern Japanese architecture, each with specific spatial qualities: concrete moment frames, geometry-specific systems, hybrid systems, solid core with light body, exoskeletons, irregular column grid, and high-tension equilibriums. Pursuing the theme of Another Nature, the project explores a new architectural language that is not simply a variation on existing structural typologies but is categorically new.

Informed by the project's civic nature, the horizontality of the context, and the brief for a new type of library as a public forum in the digital age, the proposed structural typology is a funicular system. The space follows the funicular curve, allowing a high degree of material efficiency as loads are resolved both in tension and in axis, creating space that is intimate in scale while maintaining the collective atmosphere that feels inherently public.

Compared to existing structural types, this new typology achieves a new scale of material thinness and spatial continuity. With the horizontal surfaces of floor and roof both functioning as membranes, the structure becomes something experienced not just visually but physically and directly.

I want people to enjoy the space of the library, without prescribing what they must do with it. Locally there are steep spaces, shallow spaces, low spaces, tall spaces. Overall there is a collective landscape and an awareness of a general orientation.

In using the space, which like the natural landscape has few flat surfaces, the occupants will become acutely aware of their surroundings, and senses that have grown dull in relation to the generic flatness of the city will be reactivated. Experientially, the building will recede into the background to human activities. While the spaces do not have rigidly set functions, the design provides efficient circulation and spaces suitable for a range of library activities.

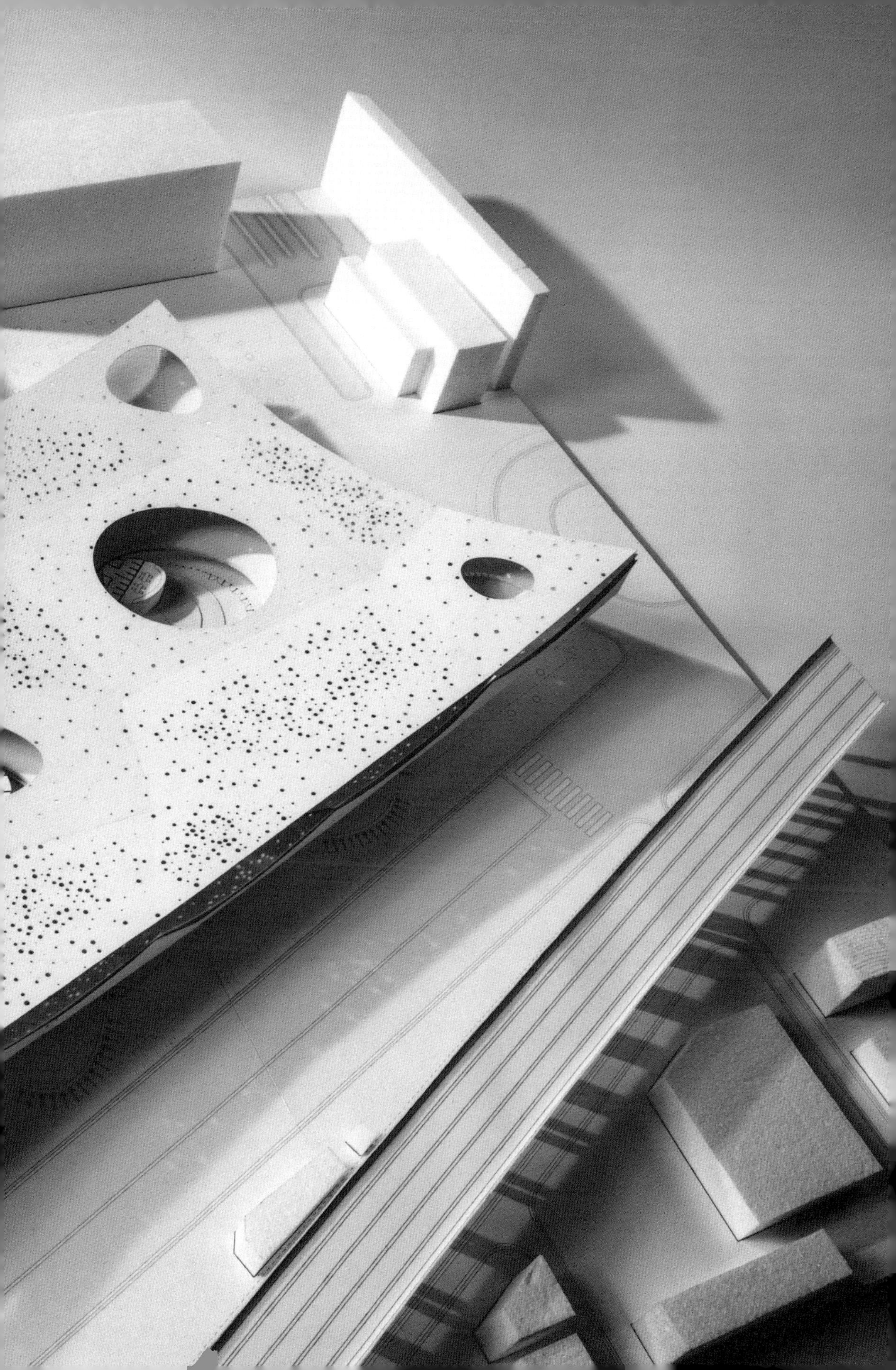

Elevated Plaza

Gunho Kim

What is public space in the reading of Another Nature? For me, Another Nature is what the structure creates and the atmosphere that the building engenders through the differentiation of conventional perceptions of space. Through the physical context, we compose an architectural space based not only on what we see but also on what we have memorized as a succession of elements. A contrast is established between what is created and what was originally present in our perception of space.

On the ground level, the structure is open to the plaza, giving easy access to the building. The elevated platform is a park as well, engaged with a park behind it through openings under the wall. But generally, although the elevated plaza is within the city, it occupies a different level, becoming a selective public space for the locals. At the top of the wall, there is an open view onto the city.

When this part of the configuration is juxtaposed on the site, it creates a plaza in relation to the neighborhood, which offers a different interpretation of public space.

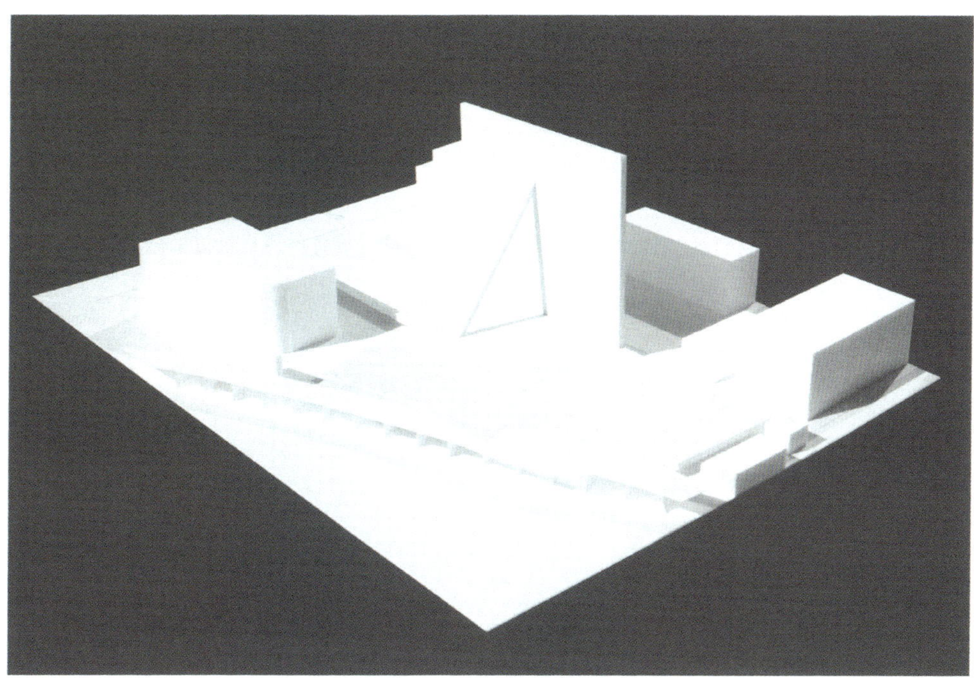

Like the plaza in front of the Seagram Building, this plaza is overshadowed by a massively tall building. As a result, the façade of the surrounding buildings are perceived as an almost infinitely continuous wall, creating a protected and introspective space for the visitor.

The wall has a giant chamber that is programmed as a cafeteria and reading space. By reaching the upper level via elevator, we find an observatory.

The diagonal structural support for the facade casts a shadow on the wall, allowing us to perceive both the shape of the wall and the passage of time.

This is a general platform structure, supported by columns and circulation. One can gain access to the plaza from everywhere on the platform.

Inside is a serene atmosphere with a curved wall.

When you look up, there is light emanating from the ceiling that gives a feeling of continuation of the wall.

528
529

Light and Shadow

Matthew Montry

Site and program—the two elements designers work with and within to derive a solution—commonly come with constraints. This project explores a system where site and program inform each other during their evolution. As the site is formed through programmatic elements, the program is informed and manipulated by the site. This embedded process, part free-form, part directed feedback loop, develops an approach to a design where the idea of site and building together become Another Nature, just as much as nature has in turn become another architecture.

The Nature of Boundaries

Quyen Luu

With inadequate open public gathering spaces and integrated public facilities, the residents of Atsugi lack opportunities to experience the sense of oneness with nature and with each other that their own city logo depicts. Another Nature is created by blurring traditionally established boundaries between human and nature, private and public, inside and outside. Combining these blurred elements yields a dialogue among them. My project is that dialogue.

Trees become walls and roofs, while walls appear fluid and transparent. Outdoor space is programmed with the same care as indoor space; buildings are programmed with the same care as landscape. Humans defer to nature, as nature and its contemplation form a guide through the space. A community is established.

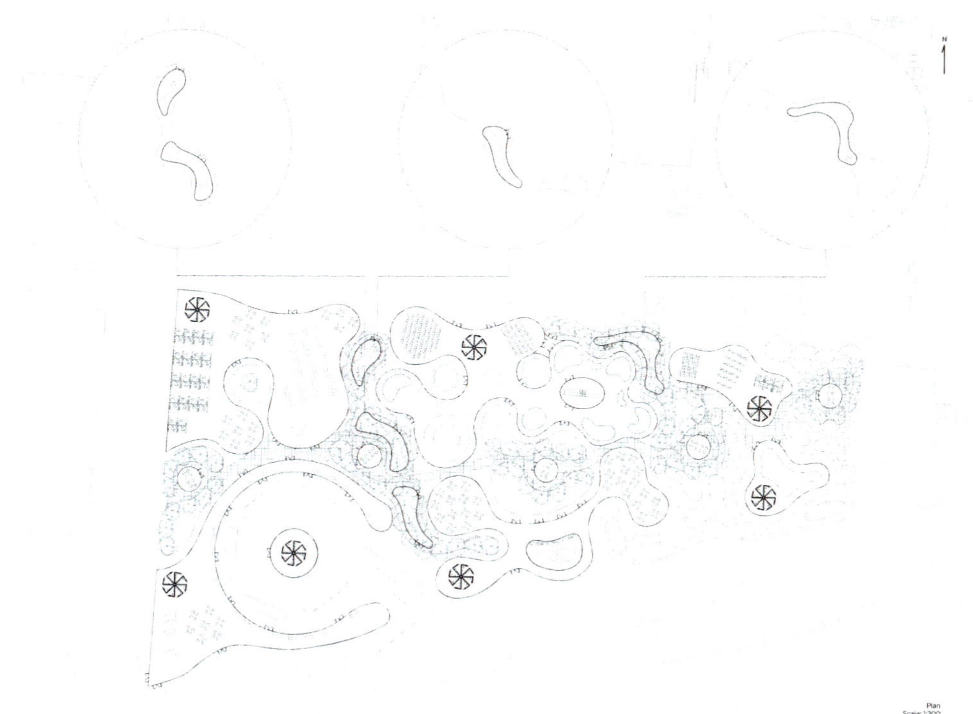

Each element forms and informs the next. At the same time, each is significant in its own right. There is no distinction as to which comes first and which follows. How can such a dialogue in turn engage in dialogue with the surrounding city? The site is a bridge between boundaries and scales, inviting the opportunity for Another Nature to form, using the same language of fragmentation.

Nature pavilions: public wayfinding devices and private nature contemplation spaces. The nature that abounds and surrounds: each green space is programmed with the same care as a building.

The community of buildings: each building is programmed with the same care as the landscape.

Stepped Civic Plaza

Yuhui Xu

In this new living environment, referred to as Another Nature, the normality of a clear boundary between inside and outside fades away, leaving architecture and nature more blended. We are used to being wrapped within the closed building envelope, isolated from the outside, especially after the invention of air conditioning. Another Nature demands breaking out from the preconception of outside and inside associated with nature and architecture. The intermediary becomes the new environment. The site in Atsugi is like an island, close yet separated from urban flows. To activate it, pinpointed architecture that deals only with the inside is not enough. The new environment should be welcoming, lively and revitalizing, connected to the urban flow, and facilitating of varied civic activities.

In the proposal, the closed building envelope unrolls to form a stepped surface that allows surface access as well as transversing circulation. An open field takes over the building blocks and provides facilities from casual seating to a small amphitheater, encouraging civic activities.

Another Nature is the redefinition of nature and architecture, a new environment where the presumption of a clear spatial boundary between them fades away. Is there a way to break out from the preconception of outside and inside associated with nature a nd architecture?

Keisai Eisen, *Cherry Blossom Picnic at Gotenyama*, ink on paper. Harvard Art Museums/Arthur M. Sackler Museum, Gift of Friends of Arthur B. Duel, 1933.4.643.

A stepped civic plaza is proposed as a new environment in the transition between outside and inside, a landscape of possible uses beyond the more specific programs as given.

Under the plaza structure are the library extension and the bus terminal.

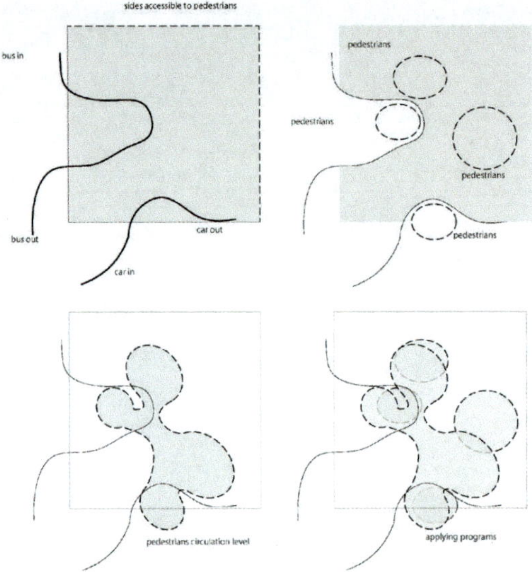

These images show the vertical layering of circulation patterns in relation to the allocation of programs. In the new environment, a free circulation pattern is proposed, with better accessibility and fewer designated pathways.

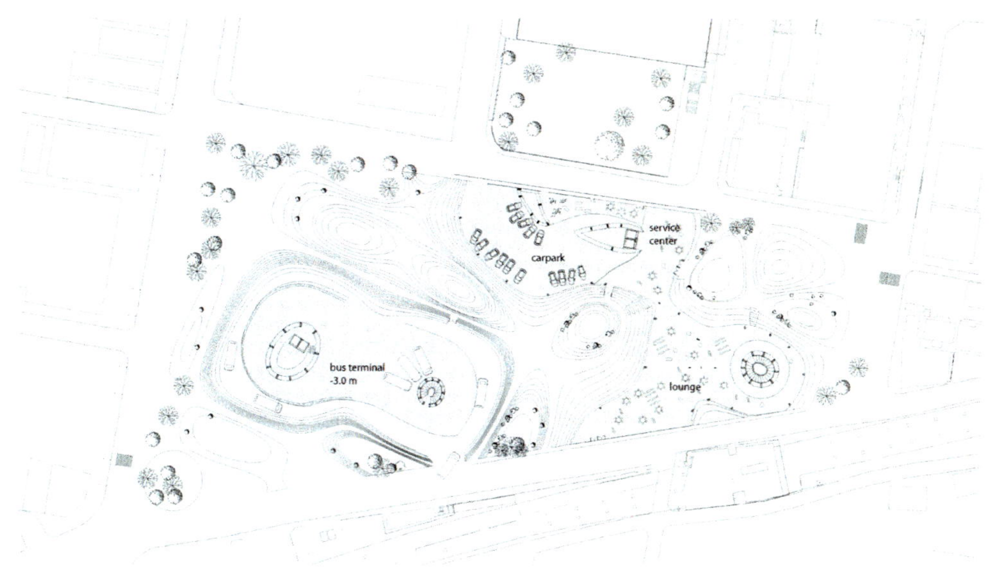

In addition to the closed small loops of individual programs, the stepped plaza creates an accessible platform that encourages interaction.

Junya Ishigami
is the founder and principal of junya.ishigami+associates in Japan. Born in Kanagawa, Japan, he graduated from Tokyo National University of Fine Arts and Music with an MFA in Architecture in 2000. That same year, he joined the office of Kazuyo Sejima & Associates. He founded his office in 2004, and in 2010 he became an associate professor at Tohoku University. The office has won several awards, including the AR Award for Emerging Architecture (2008); the Architectural Institute of Japan Prize 2009; the Bauwelt Prize 2009 for KAIT Workshop; and the Golden Lion for Best Project of the 12th Venice Architecture Biennale for "Architecture as Air: Study for Chateau la Coste" (2010).

Sky Milner
is a designer with experience living and working in Japan. He formerly worked at Atelier Hitoshi Abe in Sendai. Since 2011 he has been involved with the reconstruction efforts of Minami Sanriku with the Urban Risk Lab at MIT. He has previously taught at the Boston Architectural College and in the Harvard GSD's Career Discovery program. He is originally from Honolulu, Hawaii, and holds an MDes from the Harvard Graduate School of Design and a BArch from the Southern California Institute of Architecture.